Written by Dr. Amy West
Illustrated by Okan Bulbul

ISBN: 978-1-957922-10-2
Edition: November 2022

For all inquiries, please contact us at:
info@puppysmiles.org

To see more of our books, visit us at:
www.PuppyDogsAndIceCream.com

This book is given with love...

To: _____

From: _____

Managing Anxiety

A foreword by Clinical Psychologist, Dr. Amy West

Anxiety is a very normal (and helpful) emotion for children to experience. However, sometimes children have really strong responses to people or situations that scare them, and they start to avoid these things, which over time increases their anxiety and interferes with their ability to enjoy life. While avoiding things that scare us is a natural human instinct, it's actually quite unhelpful and makes anxiety worse.

This book presents an easy and effective approach to learning to manage anxious feelings differently – children are encouraged to identify and label the feelings they have, challenge the scary and inaccurate thoughts that feed their anxiety, and break their fears and fearful responses down into more manageable pieces. Once they have broken down their fears, children can slowly expose themselves to the things that scare them in a gradual and less overwhelming way, with new ways of thinking and new skills to understand and manage their scary feelings.

The key to overcoming unhelpful anxiety is to learn to approach, rather than avoid, the things that scare them, knowing that they can survive any challenge or obstacle on their path no matter how afraid it makes them. This is an important lesson for children and for their parents, who often unknowingly help their children avoid scary experiences because they do not want to see them suffer. Anxiety is an uncomfortable emotion, but it is not dangerous, and it often has important lessons to teach children about interacting with their world in ways that make them feel healthy and strong.

In this book, children and parents will learn that there are methods for facing anxiety that help decrease the distress and avoidance that often accompany this normal emotional experience, and ways to help children to survive and to thrive even when they feel scared!

No matter where you're standing,
If you're short or if you're tall...
You're old or young, or rich or poor,
This thing affects us all.

An uneasy sense of worry,
The concern of "what's to come?"
The thoughts that keep us up at night,
When the day at last, is done.

Anxiety is part of life,
It runs around your head.
It bounces like a pinball game,
At night, when you're in bed.

This feeling is uncomfortable,
It often makes us squirm.
But still, it serves a purpose,
From that purpose we can learn...

As weeds appear in nature,
When a garden's left to grow...
Anxiety can sprout inside,
And highlight risks to know.

Anxiety is natural,
As weeds can also be.
But if we just address it,
We can be the best we'll be.

We can choose to tend that garden,
We can pull weeds left and right.
We can let these feelings all take root,
And hide ourselves from sight.

You're old enough to know these days,
With the challenges in life...
Not everything will turn out right,
And you will encounter strife.

This worry's understandable,
It's natural to feel fear,
But let me give you some advice,
Come close, and lend an ear.

The world around you doesn't bend,
Or change itself for you.
The obstacles you come across,
Are things you must get through.

Though worries may feel difficult,
To process in your head,
There is one thing you can control,
So think of this instead...

The only thing you can control,
Is how you handle YOU.
So, take control and make a change,
Perspective will come too.

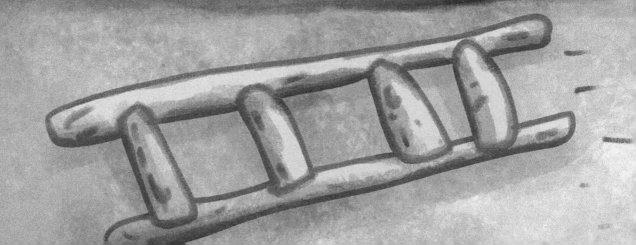

Perhaps you're feeling worried,
That some scary thing takes place...
Like being late, or tanking grades,
Or someone in your face.

Or maybe something large,
Is of concern to you...
Like asteroids, or great white sharks,
Just to name a few.

Everyone is different,
We see the world in different ways.
Our fears may take on different shapes,
Appear on different days.

The fear is real, that is certain,
But the danger may not be.
So, let's discuss just what to do,
When you feel anxiety.

STEP

1

Step one is to acknowledge,
The fear you feel with words.
It's okay to talk to someone else,
And make your worry heard.

Lay your problems out on the line,
Perhaps upon a page.
When you see them written out,
Advance to the next stage.

STEP
2

Step two is to determine,
If the worry's truly real.
Talk through the situation,
And how it makes you feel.

What exactly are the outcomes,
That you'll most likely face?
What is the chance it will occur,
That those outcomes will take place?

STEP

3

Then break it into pieces,
Just like an elephant...
They say you eat one bite by bite,
Or you won't make a dent.

Every fear feels giant,
When it's rolled up in a ball.
So, try to disassemble it,
Into pieces that are small.

STEP

4

Now you can face each piece,
Examine every one.
Step by step, address each part,
And walk before you run.

With gradual exposure,
The parts are not as huge...
And soon you'll see new avenues,
To address them and improve.

Facing something that scares you,
Builds bravery inside.
When you manage how you feel,
You'll find the fear subsides.

The world is vast and scary,
Since the dawn of time itself.
Your ancestors, too, faced their fears,
You CAN tackle them yourself.

The heroes in our stories,
Met challenges as well.
It's how they handled hurdles,
And make better tales to tell.

It's important that you focus,
On what's meaningful and real.
Don't give in to worry,
Take control of how you feel.

These emotions are all normal,
They're the start of your success.
Fear's a useful feeling,
When acknowledged and addressed.

Recognize anxiety,
As it rises from within.
Then dismantle it in pieces,
To make sure it doesn't win.

Take the opportunity,
When a challenge does arrive...
To greet your fear and say, "See here,
I'll get through this and survive!"

"I'm strong and I am willing,
To learn from this and change.
Even if it's something new,
And scary, big, or strange."

There's no limit to your bravery,
Your future's in the clear...
Once you take on challenges,
And break down all your fears.

So, take charge of how you feel,
And you will surely grow.
You're stronger than anxiety,
You're stronger than you know!

Claim your FREE Gift!

 Visit: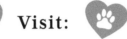

PDICBooks.com/Gift

Thank you for purchasing

Today, I Feel...

Anxious

and welcome to the Puppy Dogs & Ice Cream family.
We're certain you're going to love the little gift
we've prepared for you at the website above.

CPSIA information can be obtained
at www.ICGtesting.com
Printed in the USA
LVHW071626280323
742831LV00035B/804